T0010226

Amazing Inventions

Inventing Televisions

by Janine Ungvarsky

FOCUS
READERS®

BEACON

www.focusreaders.com

Copyright © 2022 by Focus Readers®, Lake Elmo, MN 55042. All rights reserved. No part of this book may be reproduced or utilized in any form or by any means without written permission from the publisher.

Focus Readers is distributed by North Star Editions:
sales@northstareditions.com | 888-417-0195

Produced for Focus Readers by Red Line Editorial.

Photographs ©: Shutterstock Images, cover, 1, 4, 6, 12, 14, 17, 18, 22 (TV), 25, 26, 29; itdarbs/Alamy, 8; AP Images, 11; Thomson Consumer Electronics/Herald Times/AP Images, 20–21; Unsplash, 22 (background)

Library of Congress Cataloging-in-Publication Data
Names: Ungvarsky, Janine, author.
Title: Inventing televisions / by Janine Ungvarsky.
Description: Lake Elmo, MN : Focus Readers, [2022] | Series: Amazing inventions | Includes index. | Audience: Grades 2-3
Identifiers: LCCN 2021041722 (print) | LCCN 2021041723 (ebook) | ISBN 9781637390498 (hardcover) | ISBN 9781637391037 (paperback) | ISBN 9781637391570 (ebook) | ISBN 9781637392089 (pdf)
Subjects: LCSH: Television--History--Juvenile literature.
Classification: LCC TK6640 .U54 2022 (print) | LCC TK6640 (ebook) | DDC 621.388--dc23
LC record available at https://lccn.loc.gov/2021041722
LC ebook record available at https://lccn.loc.gov/2021041723

Printed in the United States of America
Mankato, MN
012022

About the Author

Janine Ungvarsky is a former journalist who writes nonfiction for children and young adults.

Table of Contents

Chapter 1

What's On?

A boy turns on the television. The screen lights up. He clicks the remote to change the channels. There are so many choices! One channel has cartoons. Another shows a soccer game.

 A remote sends signals to a television to change the channel, volume, and more.

BREAKING NEWS   HURRICANE SLAMS COAS

LIVE NEWS

> A live broadcast gives viewers information about events right as they happen.

The boy keeps clicking. He finds a nature show about sharks. Then his mom asks him to find the weather channel. She wants to know if it will rain tomorrow. On the screen, a woman tells the forecast. She says a big storm is coming.

Next, the boy and his mom watch the news. They learn about a rocket launch. The launch is happening far away. But the news shows a **live** video of it. Then it's time to turn off the TV. There will be more to watch and learn tomorrow.

Did You Know?

In 2020, more than four billion people around the world watched television.

Chapter 2

TV History

Movies were invented in the late 1800s. And people began making radios in the early 1900s. But sending moving images over a distance was harder than sending just sounds.

 The work of many different people helped make television possible.

Early inventors tried using spinning disks. One disk had tiny holes. As the disk moved, light shone through the holes. The light made pictures on another disk. But the pictures weren't very clear.

In the 1920s, Philo Farnsworth tried a new method. Instead of disks, his television used **electrical impulses**. These impulses turned an image into lines of dots. His TV used these dots to recreate the picture. It made one line at a time.

 John Logie Baird was one inventor whose TV used spinning disks.

This system worked much better. Other inventors began using it.

Early TVs had glass screens. The glass was coated with phosphor. Phosphor glows when light hits it.

Cathode Ray Tube

Early TVs used cathode ray tubes. Each tube was shaped like a funnel. The signal came in the small end.

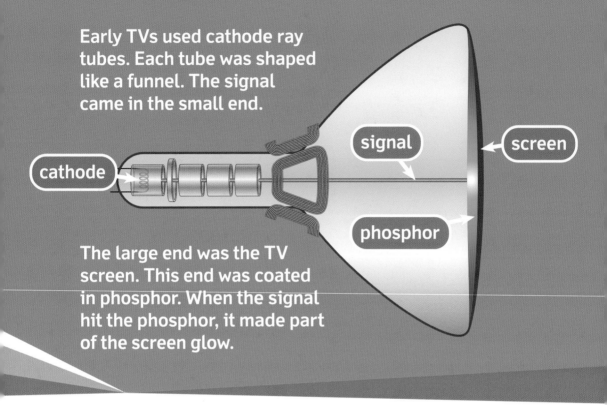

cathode

signal

screen

phosphor

The large end was the TV screen. This end was coated in phosphor. When the signal hit the phosphor, it made part of the screen glow.

The impulses hit the phosphor. It lit up to make the picture.

At first, TVs could show only black-and-white pictures. Color TVs were first sold in the 1950s. But it took more than 10 years for most shows to be made in color.

Over time, inventors made other improvements. Flat-screen TVs were invented in the 1960s. Their screens were thin and light. They also showed clearer pictures. But until the 2000s, they were too expensive for most people to buy.

Did You Know?

Philo Farnsworth was 14 when he got the idea for his television.

Chapter 3

How It Works

Television is a system for sending sounds and images. This system has three main parts. They are the camera, **transmitter**, and **receiver**. A camera picks up images. It turns them into electrical impulses.

 Sensors inside a TV camera change one line of an image into a signal at a time.

These impulses form the TV signal. Many different TV stations send signals. Each station sends its signal at a different **frequency**. That way, the signals won't mix together. Each frequency carries the sounds and images for a separate TV channel.

Did You Know?

Satellite TV sends signals to devices up in space. Those devices then send the signals back down to receivers.

A worker at a TV station helps get video ready to send out.

The signal goes to a transmitter. Transmitters send the signal to a receiver. The receiver turns the signals back into pictures. It shows them on the TV's screen.

▷ Some old TV receivers had antennas on top. Other antennas were placed on the roofs of buildings.

Some signals travel as waves in the air. The receiver's **antenna** picks them up. For cable TV, wires connect the transmitter and receiver. Signals can also be sent over the internet.

TV receivers can **display** pictures in different ways, too. Some have liquid crystal displays (LCDs). Tiny blocks on the screen turn off and on to make the picture. These blocks are called pixels. Other screens use light-emitting diodes (LEDs). The diodes shine colored lights on the screen.

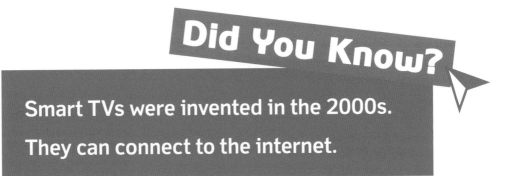

Did You Know?

Smart TVs were invented in the 2000s. They can connect to the internet.

From Knobs to Remotes

Early televisions looked different than today's TVs. They were big wooden boxes with small screens. Some screens were as small as postage stamps. Others were the size of books. The pictures were often blurry.

At first, TVs had knobs to change channels. Remotes were invented in the 1950s. A wire linked many early remotes to the TV. But some wireless remotes used light beams to change channels. Most TVs did not come with remotes until the 1980s. By the 2010s, some TVs could be controlled with cell phones.

On old TVs, one knob changed the channel. Other knobs adjusted sound or images.

AUTOMATIC SECAM-PAL 51 CTV-441 DW

Chapter 4

TV Changes

Before television, people listened to news and shows on the radio. They read newspapers, too. To see videos, people had to go to movie theaters. TVs let people watch many things from home.

By 1980, more than 95 percent of families in the United States owned a TV.

As a result, many people changed how they got news and had fun.

TV **networks** made many kinds of shows. Newspapers printed TV schedules. They listed what channel each show was on and when people could watch it. Some channels were free to watch. Others required people to pay extra.

Options could also depend on where people lived. Different places got different signals. Cable and satellite TV gave people more

 TV stations show each program at a certain time.

options. They had hundreds of channels to choose from. People often picked channels that matched their interests.

The internet brought even more changes. By 2011, people could watch many TV shows online.

Streaming services let people use the internet to watch TV shows on cell phones or computers.

Playing videos or music by sending information over the internet is called streaming. With streaming, people can choose the show they want. And they can view it at any time. Many people no longer even use TVs. They watch on other devices instead.

Many newer TVs can connect to the internet. Besides watching shows, people can visit websites, play games, and more. People have more choices than ever before.

Did You Know?

Until the 2000s, the internet was not fast enough to let people stream shows or movies.

FOCUS ON
Inventing Televisions

Write your answers on a separate piece of paper.

1. Write a paragraph summarizing the main ideas of Chapter 4.

2. What is your favorite TV show to watch? What do you like about it?

3. Which part picks up the TV signal?
    A. the camera
    B. the transmitter
    C. the receiver

4. What is one reason people might want to make thinner TV screens?
    A. Thinner screens would be easier to store and move.
    B. Thinner screens would not show colors.
    C. Thinner screens would cost more money.

5. What does **method** mean in this book?

In the 1920s, Philo Farnsworth tried a new method. Instead of disks, his television used electrical impulses.

    A. a time to sleep

    B. a plan for making money

    C. a way of doing something

6. What does **recreate** mean in this book?

His TV used these dots to recreate the picture. It made one line at a time.

    A. to stop something from happening

    B. to make something again

    C. to change how something looks

Answer key on page 32.

Glossary

antenna
A device that catches or sends radio waves or other signals.

display
To show something, often on a screen.

electrical impulses
Small bursts of electricity.

frequency
A specific type of wave used to send a signal. The speed and size of a wave affect its frequency.

live
Showing a video of something right as it happens.

networks
Companies that make and release TV shows.

receiver
A device that picks up and converts radio waves or other signals.

satellite
An object in space that orbits Earth, often to collect or send information.

transmitter
A device that sends out radio waves or other signals.

To Learn More

BOOKS

Beevor, Lucy. *The Invention of the Television*. North Mankato, MN: Capstone Press, 2018.

Bethea, Nikole Brooks. *TVs and Remote Controls*. Minneapolis: Jump!, 2021.

Kenney, Karen Latchana. *Who Invented the Television? Sarnoff vs. Farnsworth*. Minneapolis: Lerner Publications, 2018.

NOTE TO EDUCATORS

Visit **www.focusreaders.com** to find lesson plans, activities, links, and other resources related to this title.

Index

A
antenna, 18

C
camera, 15
channels, 5–6, 16, 20, 24–25

F
Farnsworth, Philo, 10, 13
flat-screen TVs, 13

I
images, 9–10, 15–16
internet, 18–19, 25–27

L
light-emitting diodes (LEDs), 19
liquid crystal displays (LCDs), 19

N
networks, 24
news, 7, 23–24

P
phosphor, 11–12
pixels, 19

R
receivers, 15–19
remotes, 5, 20

S
satellite TV, 16, 24
screens, 5–6, 11–13, 17, 19, 20
streaming, 26–27

T
transmitters, 15, 17–18
TV stations, 16

Answer Key: 1. Answers will vary; 2. Answers will vary; 3. C; 4. A; 5. C; 6. B